The story of Jesus and Mary in Kibeho

A Prophecy Fulfilled

By Immaculée Ilibagiza

Illustrated by Rupert Bazambanza

Between 1953–1964, Sister Theresa Mukamugisha, who was the Mother General of Benebekira nuns, had many visits from the Mother of God, the Virgin Mary. The Virgin gave her many different messages, among them the 7 Sorrows Rosary. The Virgin Mary asked Sister Theresa to teach others, especially the Sisters she was entrusted with. She also requested that they build a small chapel in honor of Her 7 Sorrows, which was built and still exists. Later, Sister Theresa met obstacles in spreading the message but the Virgin Mary reassured her about her continuous reappearance with the message…

It all started on November 28, 1981 early in the morning, in a boarding high school of Kibeho, Rwanda...

Wake up, it is time to pray.

When 17 year old Anathalie Mukamazimpaka, a student at the school, woke up everyone to pray, Alphonsine Mumureke (15 years old) woke up feeling anxious, with a bit of fear mixed with joy...

I feel scared.

Alphonsine went to take a shower, hoping the fear would go away...

In her classrom, she kept having a strong feeling of fear and joy...

She went to the bathroom seeking some time alone, but she felt like somebody was following her...

At lunch, it was Alphonsine's turn to serve everyone at her table…

Don't skip Anathalie, she is still praying.

At exactly 12:35pm, Alphonsine heard a voice calling her, "my child." She dropped the spoon and fell to her knees…

?

With her hands up, she answered to the voice…

Karame*!?

As if something controlled her movements, she made a sign of the cross…

In a very brilliant, beautiful light, but soft to the eye, came out a beautiful lady, young but more like a mother…

Who are you?

I am the Mother of the Word!

* Karame is a kinyarwanda word that means "Long live."

4

Students stared at her the whole time and called the nuns who were responsible for the school, to come to see…

So it is you **the mother of the Word**?

How come we don't see anyone?

1

Do you realize it is Alphonsine who was recently hospitalized over heart problems?

Maybe these are the symptoms of her sickness!

2

Among the things of God, what do you love the most?

I love God above all and the Mother who gave us the Savior!

3

If it is so, I have come to comfort you because I have heard your prayers.

I want other students to have the same faith. Because right now, they don't have enough.

4

Mother of Our Savior, if it is really you coming to remind us that we lack enough faith, you really love us. I am blessed to see you with my own eyes.

The conversation lasted about 15 minutes. When the vision ended, she collapsed on a cement floor and laid there for about 5 minutes unconscious…

This is the work of witchcraft and demons from her place of origin.

5

When she awoke, she was confused about what was going on…

What is going on? Where am I? Why are you looking at me?

The nuns asked the students to give her space and move away…

Don't be scared, you are in the dining hall, drink some water and later when you feel better, come to my office.

Marie Claire who was born in 1961, a fellow student, was convinced that Alphonsine was possessed by demons…

I am telling you, it is a bad spirit, it is not the Mother of the Word, it cannot be Mary speaking to her.

Anathalie, what do you think about this whole thing, you are a person who prays and loves God.

The more I think about it, the more I think we need to pray before we pass judgment.

In the office the director of the school Sister Germaine, whom they called Mama Germaine…

Child you were either tired or had heart problems. Please admit you didn't really see anyone, it was your imagination, this whole thing will be forgotten.

These kind of stories can hurt the church and cause serious problems.

How do you want me to say that I didn't see somebody I saw face to face? I am not crazy, I saw her with my own eyes, like I see you now.

How do you want us to explain this to the Bishop?

Why do you have to tell him? The Lady I saw only gave me a message for my fellow students.

What does she look like? How does her voice sound?

Her voice was beautiful, soft, merciful and gentle like a mother speaking to her child. Her words clear and respectful. Being in her presence made me feel loved, I never felt such peace and comfort before.

In a strange way, I felt like she was my mother I haven't seen in a long time. It felt real.

She was very beautiful, she seemed 25 years old. She was dressed like a bride, in a white veil and white dress. She was standing in a light brighter than the sun.

The Virgin Mary appeared to Alphonsine again that night, when she was alone…

Hail Mary Full of Grace, the Lord is with you…

My dear children, pray, repent and change your hearts. I will come back tomorrow after your lunch.

And keep in mind that, the message I give you, does not concern only the Diocese of Butare, Rwanda, or Africa, but the whole world.

Alphonsine kept attending class like everyone else but students watched, her every move…

If you really saw Mary, why don't you ask her to show us the answers to this exam?

The Virgin Mary came back the next day, on November 29. Alphonsine was in the dormitory…

My children, love one another, respect your educators. Be humble always and ask for forgiveness when you do wrong and forgive those who do wrong to you. Respect all God's commandments.

Why did you choose Rwanda?

Because you needed me. I also still find humble hearts who are not attached to money.

One of the students went quickly to tell the director…

Sister come quickly, Alphonsine is having an apparition again, this time in the dormitory.

Really! I am coming right away.

You want them to build a chapel for you? I will tell them but I am not sure they will listen to me. They think I am crazy, unless you appear to another student.

I wonder if this is the continuation of what was told to Sister Theresa Kamugisha!

Since the apparition in their dormitory, the students prayed around Alphonsine's bed and it became like a chapel…

We should not only pray the rosary but also wear them, because Virgin Mary said that the demons might attack those who don't wear them.

Marie Claire and her friends remained strong against Alphonsine…

I will never go to pray at Alphonsine's bed.

We have to fight against this whole thing to protect the dignity of the real Virgin Mary.

In the evening of January 12, 1982, around 7:00 p.m., Anathalie felt unwell...

I am feeling strange.

After dinner, other students went to play...

Anathalie, where are you going alone?

I feel like I want to pray.

Anathalie went to the dormitory and started to pray the rosary...

Soon she felt lost in a strange place and she saw a figure of a woman, who was very sad, it made her so sad too...

I am the Mother of God, like I said before I am the Mother of the Word.

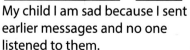

My child I am sad because I sent earlier messages and no one listened to them.

Making you cry this way, is a punishment, but it doesn't mean that you are a worse sinner than others.

It is a sign to others that I can punish them if I choose to.

Go pick the book I will show you, read the chapter you open and share your interpretation with others.

The Virgin Mary gave a blessing and left…

Anathalie what was that? What is going on with you?

Sister, please wait a minute, let me read a passage from this book, I will explain after.

The book she was asked to read is called "Immitation of Christ." Alphonsine was present…

Alphonsine, can you pray and ask Mary the meaning of what is going on with Anathalie?

Alphonsine went to pray and she held Anathalie's hands to pray together, singing "Ave Maria." At that moment, Mary came back and appeared to both of them…

Anathalie was called to the director's office to explain herself…

Anathalie, I trust you. You are a good prayerful person, honest and simple, please tell me the truth, did you really see the Mother of God?

I really saw her, but she was very sad and she said it is because we refused to accept her messages.

11

Marie Claire was very hard on Alphonsine blaming her for influencing Anathalie to lie about the apparition…

Anathalie is a good person, stop influencing her to lie about this nonsense.

One time the students were cleaning the school and Marie Claire approached Alphonsine…

I warned you and you didn't listen, wait I will show you that it hurts to be stubborn.

A few days later, Marie Claire started to openly persecute Alphonsine and throw stones at her…

Go away Satan.

Another day she puts stones and mud in her bed…

Hehehe I will make sure you lose your mind.

Alphonsine started praying for those who persecuted her, especially Marie Claire…

Mother please do something about it.

And I thank you for appearing to another student. It helped a lot, most people are now paying attention.

Besides Marie Claire, there were other students persecuting Alphonsine. One student wanted to kill her and they didn't know who it was…

One day she threw a brick at her but it didn't reach her…

Another time, she threw a knife at her and by the grace of God, it didn't catch her either…

I think this one wants to kill me.

Alphonsine was very scared but when she spoke about it, they thought she was lying. No one could see that girl…

If you care about me, I am asking you to please pray for me. I don't know what to do.

Don't worry we will pray for you.

During the apparition, some students would burn her skin to see if she felt any pain but she didn't…

Mary revealed to Alphonsine the person trying to kill her, but urged her not to tell, instead pray for her…

Many people suspected it was Marie Claire who was doing it…

I will not support anyone who wants to kill Alphonsine.

I would like to know who is responsible. It is not me.

(1)

A few days later…

Many students have started to believe and they joined Alphonsine often to pray the rosary and to dance for Mary…

♪♫ Before the valleys and mountains were created, God had you in His mind… ♫♪

(2)

As they gathered to pray, one student knelt down and apologized to Alphonsine for doing all the bad things she did…

I am the one who has been trying to kill you, please forgive me.

The Virgin Mary has told me about you.

(3)

I don't know what takes over me and compels me to do these horrible things and makes me hate you so much. I think it is the devil.

Come here. I forgive you and now let's pray for forgiveness from God.

(4)

The news reached the director of the school…

I don't want any killer in my school. You have to go back to your parents' house, I can't keep you here.

(5)

I don't think it is a good idea to dismiss her, Alphonsine forgave her and Mary who appears to her, tells us to forgive.

I forgive her but she should never do such a thing again.

(6)

Sister Germaine went to see Bishop Jean Baptiste Gahamanyi, to tell him what was going on…

I think you have come to tell me about the ongoing news of the apparitions?

I see, you have heard about it?

I already know! I know everything that happens in my diocese.

You need to be close to the girls, see how they live day to day. Write down everything they say and update me often.

If these apparitions continue, the Vatican told me that I will have to appoint a team of doctors and theologians to investigate the events.

Though they were told not to tell people, the news spread very quickly in the neighborhood and the entire country…

It is a secret, don't tell anyone.

They see and talk to the Mother of God. She called herself the Mother of the Word.

The whole country seemed to be talking about it…

How is that possible?

Have you ever heard of anyone coming from heaven to speak to people on earth?

Mary the mother of Jesus who died a long time ago? We have to go to see for ourselves.

I will believe when I see.

During different apparitions to Alphonsine and Anathalie, Mary referred to people as Her Flowers…

The sisters called Marie Claire and asked her to stop persecuting other girls…

Stop persecuting Alphonsine and Anathalie, you can't pretend to know the plans of God.

Marie Claire accepted the advice of the sisters but she was not happy. She started to pray asking the real Virgin Mary to intercede and stop Alphonsine…

Marie Claire started seeing things she couldn't explain. For example her clothes would be found teared up. Other students thought it was the bad spirits doing it…

On March 1, 1982, Marie Claire and her friend were walking in the garden looking at tomatoes the students planted…

Marie Claire felt like she was in another place, she couldn't see her friend anymore. The place where she was, smelled really bad…

Marie Claire started running away from the smelly place, she was running to a place where Alphonsine had the apparitions, near her bed, a place she had vowed to never go…

Marie Claire said she was seeing ugly men, like monsters running after her, wanting to hurt her…

Please help me, please help me.

Those who saw her said she was in pain and convulsing on the ground…

These are demons! Mary told Alphonsine that they will attack those who don't wear the rosaries.

At night, Marie Claire went to write a letter to her parents telling them about the terrible things she was experiencing…

Those monsters came back angry and screaming, asking her to give them a sacrifice…

HELP, HELP!

I sent you people and things, and you are too difficult, we are leaving but we will come back anytime.

Marie Claire and Anathalie were studying in the same class. It was March 2, 1982…

Anathalie says that Mary is coming to visit her, anyone who would like to be there, please go.

Marie Claire, why don't you go?

When Anathalie started to give blessings to the rosaries, Marie Claire felt like she was in another place where the light was very bright, warm and perfect…

She heard a gentle voice of a woman calling her by name and she thought it was the bad guys coming back. She refused to answer…

Marie Claire

Marie Claire

Marie Claire

①

A moment after…

I am awake

Why are you scared?

I thought it was the bad guys coming back. Sorry.

②

Those things that scare you, will not come back. The voice asked her to sing a song called, "Blessed are those who are persecuted for righteousness"…

Marie Claire didn't like singing, so she approached Anathalie the only one she could see and they sang together…

③

Students who heard that Marie Claire had an apparition, were very surprised…

What? Marie Claire had an apparition?

I guess everyone is going to have an apparition.

④

Even Alphonsine who had been praying for Marie Claire was shocked, she didn't expect that…

Thank you dear Mother

⑤

The news spread all over and people started to go to see what was happening…

Virgin Mary, if it is you, please help our brothers and sisters, the Tutsis refugees to come back home.

People tried everything to see the girls, they even tried to look through the windows of the school to see the visionaries…

I can't see them.

Sister Germaine was not happy and she tried to chase the people away…

Go away from the school, you can't do this, it is against the law.

We heard Mary is appearing here and we are not leaving without seeing the girls who see Her.

The Parish priest who was near came to see what was happening…

We will not be able to manage these people if we don't let them see the girls and be present at the apparitions.

What can I do? The Virgin Mary doesn't always say the time and day She is coming.

Sister Germaine and the priest agreed to seek permission from the Bishop to build a podium outside where everyone could see the girls. They also asked the girls to ask Mary if She would meet them outside…

Can you ask Mary?

Yes we will ask Her.

When Bishop Gahamanyi heard there were more girls having apparitions, he notified the Vatican…

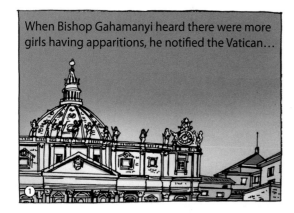

The church then was led by Pope Jean Paul II, and he immediately sent a theologian commission to investigate…

Mary agreed to meet the girls outside and the bishop issued an order to build a podium where Mary would meet them…

The podium was built with wood and they put a lot of grass on the ground to protect the girls, because at the end of every apparition they lost consciousness and collapsed to the ground…

The bishop is putting together a commission to watch the girls day and night to help him understand what is going on.

All we want is to know the truth, as long as the girls are protected. Besides, these unusual events, the girls are good, normal kids.

Soon Marie Claire had another visit by Mary…

Mother, I have never seen that kind of rosary.

My dear child, this is the rosary of my 7 Sorrows!

I want you to learn it and to teach it to other people.

①

How am I going to learn it? Nobody knows it.

②

Tell my children, that whoever prays this rosary sincerely, they will receive visible graces. To those they will pray for, I will bless them as if they prayed it themselves. Hearts of stone will soften. Problems that seemed to have no answers before, will be answered. Parents who will pray it for their children, I will hear them in a special way.

Pay attention to what I am about to show you.

③

Mary taught her first, her sufferings. Marie Claire watched as if it was a movie, she did not know it was Mary and Jesus in the story…

1. The prophecy of Simeon…

?

Why did that man say sad things to that woman? Oooh!

What is her child going to suffer from?

④

21

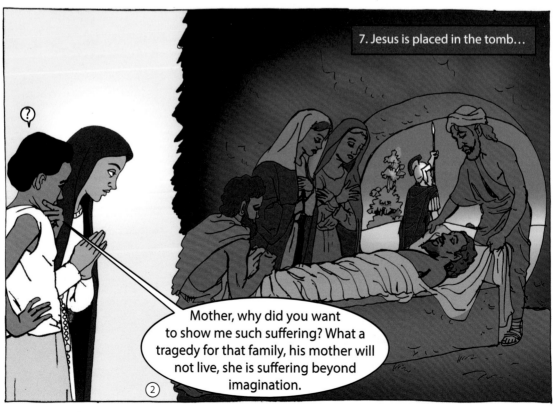

People who were watching saw Marie Claire with an unusual rosary in her hands, but they didn't know where it had come from…

Sign of cross + Beginning Prayer:

1: My God I offer you this Rosary for your Glory and to honor your Holy Mother Mary, so I can share and meditate upon her suffering. I humbly beg you to bring me to true repentance for all my sins. Give me wisdom and humility so that I may receive all the indulgences from this prayer.

2: Act of Contrition

3: 3 Hail Mary's

4: Most Merciful Mother, remind us always about the sorrows of your Son Jesus.

5: 1st Sorrow…

6: Our Father…

7: 7 Hail Mary's

8: Most Merciful Mother…

9: 2nd Sorrow…

10: 7 Hail Mary's and so on…

11: Closing prayer:

Queen of Martyrs, your heart suffered so much. I beg you, by the merits of the tears you shed in those terrible and sorrowful times, to obtain for me and all the sinners of the world, the grace of complete sincerity and repentance.

12: 3 times say, "Mary who was conceived without sin and who suffered for us, pray for us."

Marie Claire's personality changed to a point that everyone could see it. She spent time praying and teaching her fellow students the 7 Sorrows Rosary…

Like Anathalie and Alphonsine, she gave a good example and helped those in need. For example they volunteered to wash clothes for students who were sick…

One time Alphonsine was praying with her friends…

Mary said she will come to take me to show me something. She said I will appear dead, but my soul will be with her.

Alphonsine told the director of the school Sister Germaine when she will go with Mary…

On March 20, 1982, Alphonsine went to her bed…

Students said bye to her by singing Mary's songs…

Alphonsine laid on the bed, and she fell unconscious. She appeared dead…

Virgin Mary came and took her soul with her…

Alphonsine was unusually heavy. One time, she almost fell off the bed. The sisters tried to move her in vain. They called a few men to help them, without much success…

After a few hours without moving, they thought she was dead, they called a doctor…

She is alive.

Amen.

When Alphonsine woke up, she found everyone staring at her, and she was confused…

Alphonsine told them about the trip she had just come from with the Virgin Mary…

It was as if we were sliding, but I couldn't tell if we were going up or down. Not much effort was made. It was all easy.

The first part we saw was very bad, ugly, there was a lot of misery. There I saw people in terrible pain. They were fighting, extremely angry…

Who are those people?

They are those who will suffer eternally, those who will never be forgiven.

The second part they visited was a place that had a little light, not so pleasant. They were suffering a lot, but not like in the first part. They seemed patient, they were looking upward where they seemed to be expecting something or somebody who could help them…

These are those who will be forgiven, who will be chosen.

The third part had a very beautiful light. The light was brighter than the sun, but it doesn't look like the light of the sun. It was not cold or hot, the light was gentle, pure perfection. There I could hear beautiful voices…

Here is a dwelling place of those who have light in their hearts. The place of those who respect God.

I hear beautiful singing voices but I don't see people.

You can't see these people before you leave earth.

There she heard voices asking her to deliver messages to people she knew on earth…

One voice said…

Is it you Alphonsine who saw the Mother of God? Me too when I was on earth I saw her, and I was persecuted for that. I was put in prison, and my parents were persecuted saying that they didn't take me to a psychiatrist. You will also suffer, but always remember you are with the Mother of God who will always be there for you.

The voice continued…

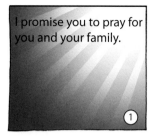

I promise you to pray for you and your family.

①

Why did you show me all that?

②

I showed you those 3 parts so that you know the life that matters most, is what is coming after this life on earth. Go and tell everyone, encourage them to live the right way. Tell them that to live without respecting God, is the ultimate waste of time, they will regret it bitterly.

It is time for you to go now.

Please let me stay here

My child, it is not time yet, for now things have to be so.

③

Alphonsine did not want to leave, she cried…

This is what you will tell the Sisters who take care of you.

④

Tell them that they must love the rosary. The 7 Sorrows Rosary and the Traditional Rosary. Tell them to say it with their hearts, being conscious of who they are talking to. Tell them to ask for the strength to help them accomplish the promises they made to God…

The Virgin Mary continued…

Remind them to always show love to each other, so that others will take good example from my daughters. Tell them to be a true reflection of my love to everyone they meet, everywhere they go, imitating my behavior and virtues. ⑤

It is then that I came back…

⑥

The 3 men who saw what happened, were shocked, and went to visit Bishop Jean Baptiste Gahamanyi right away to tell him…

Alphonsine was very heavy, we couldn't move her. A little girl of 95 pounds heavy, all of us, 3 men, we tried to lift her in vain.

This situation is beyond my understanding.

⑦

On the evening of March 20, 1982, the Bishop established a commission of investigators of the apparitions. He selected the best doctors in the country who will follow up on those events and report back to him…

⑧

Among the doctors who were sent to Kibeho, there were physicians, psychiatrists, internists, anesthetists, etc…

⑨

28

On March 27, 1982, there was a rumor of an imminent apparition. Many people came but the girls were not aware beforehand…

There is no apparition, go home.

You are not listening to me, there is no apparition today.

People did not believe the Sister, they refused to leave. Around 5:00 p.m., everyone outside was suprised to see an unusual strong light from the place of the apparition…

When asked later, a few people only saw a small light like the one shed by insects…

That night Mary appeared unannounced to Marie Claire…

Hail Mary…I didn't know you were coming today.

I didn't want to disappoint my children who have been waiting for me outside. The star they saw is a sign from me and a light for those who needed it.

Thank you, dear Mother.

The investigators of the church started working intensively to see if these events were supernatural or not, and if so, if they are from God or else…

Whenever they were talking to Mary, the girls couldn't feel anything from outside. The doctors poked their eyes with needles but the girls did not blink at all…

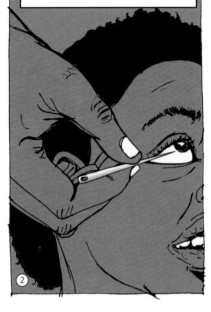

They injected needles in their feet and they did not react…

The theologians appointed by the church, recorded every message to analyze if there was anything that contra-dicted the teachings of the Church in them…

After the events, the commission met regularly to discuss and evaluate every message…

The commission was tasked to report to the Bishop, who in turn, will report to the Vatican…

Something wonderful is happen-ing in our midst.

As the months passed into a new year, the words of Mary started changing. They seemed urgent, calling people to change to avoid bitter consequences…

The world is falling apart because people don't have enough love.

Marie Claire was also told similar words…

There is a lot of hatred, jealousy, people committing sins without much care, there is not much peace among people.

Like Anathalie…

The world is going bad my child, if your hearts don't change, you will all perish.

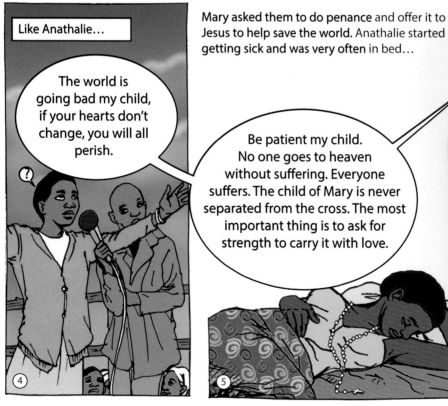

Mary asked them to do penance and offer it to Jesus to help save the world. Anathalie started getting sick and was very often in bed…

Be patient my child. No one goes to heaven without suffering. Everyone suffers. The child of Mary is never separated from the cross. The most important thing is to ask for strength to carry it with love.

It was in May that Mary told Anathalie that school was not her calling. She was sad because she loved school…

It is not your calling.

Mary came back and repeated it to her…

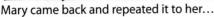

You will suffer my child but you will help me to save many souls. I will give you joy, but you will have to accept sufferings as well. Also, I am asking you to stay in Kibeho until I tell you otherwise. I chose you for a difficult task.

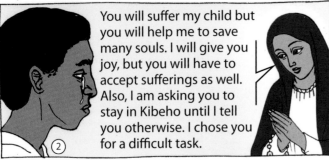

Anathalie kept going to school. One time, she tried to study for an exam…

Should I study or not? She didn't tell me when I should stop.

When she opened one notebook, she saw a strange handwriting in a different color she had never seen before…

TRUST THAT I AM WITH YOU ALWAYS

She got scared…

She opened another notebook…

IN YOUR SUFFERING, MANY ARE SAVED

Any notebook she took, there were new writings and a new message…

THE PLANS I HAVE FOR YOU ARE NOT DONE YET

It did not stop…

GO AND WRITE EVERYTHING I TELL YOU, ESPECIALLY THOSE THINGS THAT YOU THINK WILL HELP OTHERS

Dear Mother, I am done with school

Panel 1

The month of May was also the month when new visionaries were heard from outside of the school. There was Valentine Nyiramukiza who was born on Dec. 25, 1972. She had the first apparition on May 15, and she continues to have apparitions every year, on the same date…

Panel 2

Hail Mary Full of Grace and Mother of the Word

Remember to pray without ceasing, love one another, be simple and humble and mortify yourself for your sins and the sin of others

Panel 3

The message I entrust to you is to pray for the sick and those who are oppressed and possessed by demons. You will also suffer, in order to help my Son to save souls.

Panel 4

Like other visionaries there was mysterious things during Valentine's apparitions…

My child, receive this oil that you will use to anoint people who wish to be anointed and it will protect them from bad spirits.

Panel 5

The oil came into her hands in front of everyone. What they couldn't see, was where it was coming from. It was stored in bottles after…

This is a miracle.

?

?

Mary taught Valentine songs and sometimes she would dance for her and teach her...

You know how to dance like us Rwandans, you dance beautifully.

When you dance for God, you are praying. Dance with the heart, with gentleness and purity. Thinking of the words you are dancing to and who you are dancing for.

People watched Valentine dancing and imitating Mary, as she kept admiring how Mary danced so gently and beautifully...

Valentine also had apparitions of Jesus. He repeated what Mary told her...

Remember to pray, love one another, be simple, humble yourself, mortify yourself for your sins and those of your brothers and sisters.

There was another girl of 14 years old who also said she saw Mary. Her name was Stephanie Mukamurenzi...

Her first apparition was on May 25, 1982 when she was in church praying...

Her main mission was to pray and remind people to pray for those who criticize the things of God...

What is she still doing in the church this long?

Let me go and see.

34

Stephanie was asked by Mary to meet her on the podium they built in Kibeho, the general apparition place...

There are people who gave me messages for you. Can I tell you?

Tell them to speak to me directly, I will listen to them.

I came toward you and my message was not well received, it was mocked and turned into jokes.

The journalists from around the world came to Kibeho to see what was happening. The investigators of the church never stopped trying to verify if this was really supernatural or not...

During the apparitions they flashed blinding lights in their faces. They did not blink once, and yet, outside of the apparition, they blinked...

The doctors even tried dangerous ways. They were seen trying to strangle the kids during apparitions and the kids continued to speak normally. Outside of the apparition, they lost their breath and fainted...

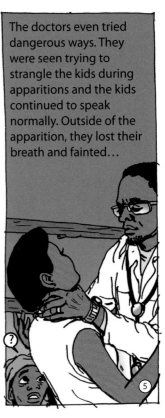

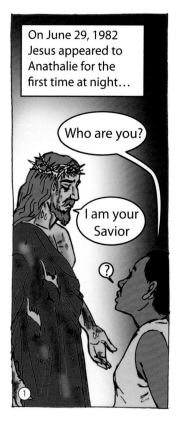

On June 29, 1982 Jesus appeared to Anathalie for the first time at night…

Who are you?

I am your Savior

That day He came looking very sad, like he was during His passion on earth. Oct. 24, He appeared to her again…

You look very sad

He showed her the wounds on His body…

Anathalie had various temptations. There were people who asked her to leave Kibeho and go on vacation with them against Mary's instructions…

My family is rich we will take good care of you.

No, Mary told me to stay here

One of the things she did often was to receive people's rosaries and offered them to Mary to bless them…

Many times she asked Mary to bless the water people brought to Kibeho. Mary told us to use holy water often to protect ourselves from bad spirits…

July 1982, Anathalie started a new thing. She started going to pray outside in the forest at night upon request of Mary. She told her she wanted to teach her about suffering, praying for herself and for others…

She said many prayers in the forest, the Traditional Rosary and the 7 Sorrows Rosary. Whenever she went to pray, a big animal attacked her and scared her, but Mary told her to be strong and finish her prayers…

Pray, pray a lot, repent your sins and change your hearts. Forgive one another and know how to apologize to one another. I love you my children. Love your parents and obey them. When I tell you to change, I don't mean you alone but all people. Remind people to respect ALL God's commandments.

A day that will never be forgotten was the Assumption, August 15, 1982! That day, 5 children saw Mary one after another. Mary stayed for 8 hours. From 3:00 p.m. until 11:00 p.m. The students were on vacation, but the visionaries stayed. There were over 30,000 people present…

Though it was a feast, Mary appeared very sad, with tears in her eyes. The kids who saw her seemed to be suffering as well…

Why did you show me your tears Mother?

Why do you refuse to talk to me and cry?

Sing for me this song ♫ people have betrayed me! ♫

Mary repeated 3 times "I opened and they refused to come in, I opened and they refused to come in, I opened and they refused to come in." Then she showed her a river of blood…

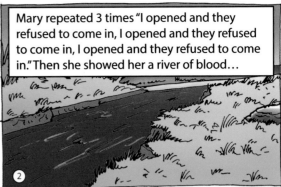

She showed her houses on fire all around a mountain. She showed her people killing each other. She showed many dead bodies and decapitated heads…

She showed Anathalie a big hole where people stand right at the edge of it. Mary told her that she can't be happy seeing the danger her children are in…

Mother, please help us not to fall in that hole.

People who were there on August 15, were scared by the words Mary told the children and what they were seeing…

If you don't want to listen now, you will wish to listen when it is too late.

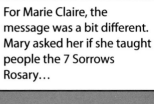

For Marie Claire, the message was a bit different. Mary asked her if she taught people the 7 Sorrows Rosary…

Mother, they won't believe your messages because they think I'm crazy!

Marie Claire listened for a while and she started crying inconsolably…

Then she repeated 7 times…

I give myself totally to you Mother, you give all graces, do whatever you want of me so people can listen and be saved.

Marie Claire saw herself in a field of thorns, she fell inside and they pierced her skin…

Please have mercy on people.

Another person that saw Mary that day was Valentine…

Have mercy on us, we are weak.

Stephanie also had apparitions that night. She cried very much looking at the sadness of Mary…

Why are you so sad Mother?

40

September 4, 1982 Mary visited Anathalie and talked to her about the Chapel she requested to be built…

They told me that they don't know how big you want it, and they don't know where you want it to be built.

(1)

Mary told her to come down and she will show her where she wanted it and how big she wanted it…

I need a chapel here that will be a memory of my many visits. I want it to be a place where everyone in the world will come to pray and will praise their God. Here, I will hear those who are suffering and heal many hearts.

(2)

Mary showed her where she wanted the 2 Chapels. The big one and the small one. Anathalie went around the field counting steps. The investigators of the church followed her and put signs…

? ? ? ? ?

1, 2, 3, 4…

(3)

She went all around the field and counted steps up to 60 meters for the big one and up to 30 meters for the small one…

(4)

On May 19, 1982, Mary showed Anathalie the full Chapels already built…

It is so beautiful. Never saw anything like that.

That is how I want them to be. They can't make them exactly like that, but tell them what you saw, they will try.

(5)

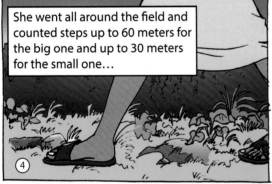

Mary told her to call the big chapel "IYEGERANYA RY'ABATATANYE," which means "A REUNION OF THE DISPERSED." The small one will be called the "CHAPEL OF THE SEVEN SORROWS." The Chapels were decorated by beautiful statues as she described them…

(6)

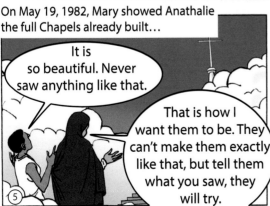

Outside of the school were a few more people who said they had apparitions, too. For example, Vestine Salima who was born in 1958…

It was July 1980, she heard a voice of Mary speaking to her…

In the days ahead, you will teach many who will come to you.

Then she saw a man bringing her books…

You are bringing those to me? Who are you?

I am Jesus the Son of God the Father.

I am sending you to teach many people, and you will always carry a staff in your hands, a sign of a shepherd.

When Salima came to Kibeho, they were surprised that she was Muslim…

I am a Muslim but Jesus told me to join a prayer group here.

Salima had her first apparition of Mary in Kibeho September 15, 1982…

Salima was given the mission to remind people to pray with the heart and willingness…

Ask people why are they not making an effort to pray to their God?

Tell them that I see their hearts far away, why?

There came another visionary, a boy whose name was Segatashya…

My name is Segatashya and I see Jesus who gives me a message for people.

The boy was a pagan, he had never gone to school. He didn't know anything about God…

His main message was to remind people that the world will end, and that Jesus will come back to take the good for eternal reward and send the bad to eternal damnation…

To remind people that they don't know when they will die and that they should always stand ready. To tell people how the end of the world will unfold.

If anyone knows that I ever set foot on earth, let them know that I am on my way back.

In the last days there will be many troubles. The good and the bad will suffer.

Segatashya was invited by Jesus to meet on the podium like other visionaries…

The day I will come back, I will send my angels to the 4 corners of the world to gather all people.

They will separate the bad from the good. Change your hearts while there is still time, because the days that remain are numbered.

43

One time Jesus introduced Mary to him. He told him he wants to show him somebody who is very special…

This is my mother

Wow! You are so beautiful!

How is it possible for anyone to look like this? She is so pure and peaceful like a dove.

I want you to love her as you love yourself and to respect her as you respect me.

Jesus asked Segatashya to give a message to priests who were in a conference…

Jesus appreciates what you do but He said that when you work for God, you don't play.

He told me to tell you to change your hearts while there is still a chance. He asks you why you don't respect the promises you made to Him?

Some of you commit the sin of adultery. He sees you when you remove your crosses and go to political meetings that kill people. Why you don't love each other? Stop following many paths. Follow the one true path.

There were those who left the room angry, saying that Jesus can't talk to them like that…

Jesus gave Segatashya the message to go to share in other countries. First, He sent him to Democratic Republic of Congo but he didn't get a visa to go, and he didn't speak their language either. Jesus asked him to go anyway that He will be with him…

Here I am at the border what am I going to do?

As he is asking himself what to do next. He saw a car that stopped near him and when he looked he knew the person who was driving the car. It was a business man he met in Kibeho. He offered to drive him across the border…

This man was known and when he reached the border of DR Congo-Rwanda, they opened quickly without asking…

He also found a family that knew him and proposed him to host him. They tried to teach him the language but it was too hard…

Segatashya when are you getting married?

Jesus told me that I will not reach the age He was when He died, so it is not necessary to get married knowing that.

A week later he started preaching in public, giving the message Jesus gave him to give people. But he had a translator…

This man is saying things I didn't say.

Segatashya started right away to speak in the native language of Congo, Swahili, only after a week…

Why is he using a translator when he can speak perfect Swahili? Without even an accent.

Segatashya continued to share the message Jesus gave him…

Jesus asks you to respect all God's commandments. One sin can have many sins in it. Jesus reminds you to change your hearts when there is still time.

Follow His commandments as they are. A man who has another woman besides the one who was given to him, is an adulterer and he is a murderer like any other murderer because he is killing the peace of his wife. He is also a thief like any thief because he is stealing what was not given to him by the law and by God.

Jesus said to that man if he doesn't change, he will fall into hell.

A woman who is with a man who is not hers, that woman is also an adulterer, she is a murderer like any other murderer and she is a thief like any other thief.

I have children from a man who is married to another woman, he is the one who feeds my children, so what do you want me to do? It is too late for me to stop!

If you love that man, and you love yourself, let go of that man, don't sin with him, give peace to his wife. Jesus will take care of you…

If he wants he will continue to help his children but he must do it in harmony with his wife.

Many people were angry with this message that was not easy for them to accept and change…

Me too, I have 3 women and all of them have my children, will that be Christian to reject them?

To love your children and to love those women is not to sin with them. You were given one woman by God, nothing more. Take care of your children but you must do it with the understanding and help of your wife, don't sin.

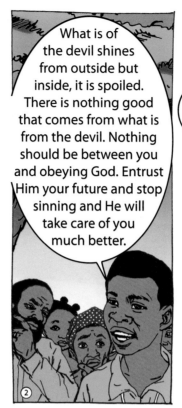

Another visionary came in the picture. Agnes Kamagaju saw Jesus on August 4, 1982…

Her main message was to help those who are not strong in their faith and to pray for the youth. There were signs in the sky during her apparitions…

Young people must respect their bodies, avoid the sin of adultery. One mistake can weigh heavily on the future.

There was a time her whole body lifted from the ground about 9 centimeters…

Change your hearts.

There was a time everyone saw a big cross in the sky…

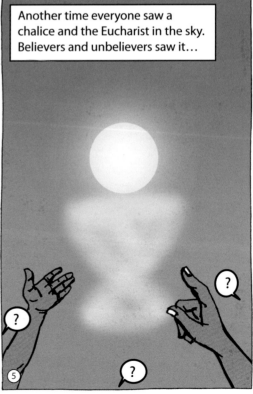

Another time everyone saw a chalice and the Eucharist in the sky. Believers and unbelievers saw it…

October 23, 1982 Jesus came to visit Anathalie...

Who are you?

Anathalie my child

I am your Savior.

Why don't you look like last time.

I came with my body when I was suffering. You see you are not the only one who suffers on earth. You saw how many Saints suffered, no one goes to Heaven without suffering. Even me I suffered on earth before I went to Heaven.

You look happy today!

I wanted to show you that those who accept their sufferings with love on earth, will one day be very happy in Heaven where there is no more pain.

So what can I do to get to Heaven?

To go to Heaven, you must respect God's commandments and put them in practice. You have to distinguish yourself by strong love of God and of people. And you must accept God's Will in everything...

So you came to teach me that?

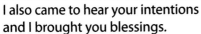

I also came to hear your intentions and I brought you blessings.

Jesus also explained to Anathalie the benefits of fasting...

Fasting helps to save souls and to resolve a lot of problems. I spent 40 days and nights fasting when I was on earth.

Similar to Alphonsine, Mary took Anathalie to visit life after this. She told people that she will look dead but to not bury her, she will come back…

They sat around her all night. She looked like she was in a coma…

She woke up after 7 hours and she said that Mary told her not to speak for 2 days meditating on what she saw before she spoke about it…

Finally she spoke…

The first part we saw was very beautiful. It had a brilliant light, very nice to look at and to be around. There were 7 people…

What is this place Mother?

It is called Isangano*

Who are those people and what do they do?

They are angels, their job is to praise God and to come to the help of people.

There were many people, people who were in line and you couldn't see where the line started or ended. They were almost all of the same age and they were more than happy…

What is this place and who are those people?

This is a place of fulfillment of joy.

Those are the cherished of the Almighty.

We went to another place that had light but not as good, not enough light. People were also in line, but they were in pain. They were in order, very patient…

Who are those people? Where is this place?

It is a place of purification and those people are those who don't get tired.

*Isangano: A place of where everything meets.

The 4th part: We arrived in a very ugly place. There was no light, it was hot beyond bearing. People wore dark clothes. They were in such pain and suffering, I never imagined it would be possible…

Where is this place and who are those people?

This is a place of punishment. Those who don't listen.

At the end of the visit…

Go and meditate on the 3 parts of people I showed you last. It shows how people are on earth. They are those who love God always and are good even if they are not perfect. They are those who pray sincerely only when they are going through difficult times. And they are those who have hearts of stones. Pray for all of them.

Tell people what you saw and tell them that the body lives on earth but the spirit lives eternally. Don't spend time caring more for the body that will live a short time, rather care for the spirit that will live forever.

As time went on, people started to change their hearts slowly because of the apparitions in Kibeho, which they called bearing fruits for Mary…

People brought water for the Virgin Mary to bless it for them. Those who were early had a chance to place the water on the podium…

That day it was Anathalie who had an apparition first…

Hail Mary…

Go and help me water my garden of flowers.

You have many flowers. But some are beautiful, others are weak and others are dry. Should I water them all?

I love my flowers all the same. Water them the same. I have hope that the dry can become beautiful anytime. And I water the beautiful ones because they can dry as well. Open your arms on the water so I can give them a blessing.

She came down and walked through people splashing water on them…

There were also those to whom she gave to drink as per Mary's wish…

When there were too many people and the garden was too big, sometimes Mary helped them by making a rain of blessing fall over them. It was a miracle everyone experienced…

Anathalie started an unusual fasting, of 14 days without eating or drinking…

During 14 days, Anathalie only received the Eucharist in the morning. Before she received it, she spent time in prayer…

In 1983 Anathalie started a new thing, during apparitions she prayed over people and there were many physical and spiritual healings…

At every apparition, Anathalie gave Mary's blessings to the water…

Mary used all visionaries in the same manner during their apparitions…

To work for Heaven is not easy, but if you make an effort, you will always receive help.

On August 15, 1988 the bishop Jean Baptiste announced that yes miracles do happen in Kibeho, and it should be a place of public worship. He gave permission to celebrate masses there. After consideration of the commission reports, he concluded to consider and follow up only 9 visionaries out of 50 who claimed to have apparitions as well…

Thank you for a great job. May God bless you.

On November 28, 1989 the Virgin Mary appeared to Alphonsine for the last time in public. She prepared her for two years for that day. Alphonsine cried a lot and told Mary that she doesn't think she can make it without seeing Her anymore. People who watched her crying were also very sad…

The Virgin Mary came for the last time in public…

You really come to say bye to me my sweet Mother? I can die of sadness. How am I going to live without you?

My child, I told you all I needed to tell you, I am not leaving you, I will be near you always. Don't be sad.

I pray for all people who need you Mother, I pray for the Church and its future. I offer you the children.

If you follow the Gospel of my Son, you will always be happy in your Souls.

For Anathalie, the **Virgin** Mary said **bye** to her on December 3rd, 1983. She cried a lot as well…

Marie Claire's apparitions lasted about 6 months. Her last visit was September 15, 1982. She cried inconsolably…

In 1990, Pope Jean Paul II visited Rwanda and he was welcomed by many people who already prepared by Mary's visits in Kibeho...

Welcome to Rwanda Papa Jean Paul II!

Welcome we love you!

Peace of Jesus Christ be with you.

Welcome to Rwanda our dear Pope!

Remember to always call upon Our Mother Mary to protect you. Love one another, let your tribes be a reason to appreciate the work of God. Remember He created each human being in His image. Don't let there be a reason to hate each other.

The Pope also had a private meeting with the Bishop Jean Baptiste Gahamanyi...

You are so blessed to have Kibeho, take good care. And please pray for me.

Apart from internal frustrations and divisions, Rwanda had more than a million Tutsi Refugees outside the country who were denied to come back to the country for 30 years. There was a lot of frustrations and suffering among them. Mary knew the danger we were in and she tried to help us love one another, accept one another, but we did not listen. It had just started.

On October 1990, RPF* Inkotanyi, declared a war as an effort to force the government to accept the refugees…

(1)

Tutsis refugees…

(2)

The government of Juvenal Habyarimana then created a group called "Interahamwe" and they were trained to kill…

(3)

The goal of that group was to kill all the Tutsis who were left in the country, so they could discourage the FPR from bringing back the refugees…

(4)

After a few months, the government in power realized that the RPF that was led by Major Paul Kagame, was strong so they agreed to negotiate a peace treaty to bring them back…

(5)

To facilitate the negotiations, the United Nations sent a mission of civilians and soldiers to Rwanda (UNAMIR*). The military group was led by Romeo Dallaire…

(6)

The signing of the peace agreements took place in Arusha Tanzania. The president of the country then shook hands with the leader of the political party of the RPF…

(7)

Colonel Theoneste Bagosora in the government of Juvenal Habyarimana, did not like the peace agreements to bring back the Tutsis refugees…

I am going to prepare an apocalypse of Tutsis. A war that will eliminate every single one of them.

(8)

* RPF Inkotanti: (Rwandan Patriotic Front). A political party that was created by Tutsis refugees.
* UNAMIR: United Nations Assistance Mission for Rwanda.

Finally we found out what made Mary cry on August 15, 1982…

On April 6, 1994, 2 years after the two parties signed the peace agreement, the plane of the President Juvenal Habyarimana was shot on his way back from Arusha, Tanzania…

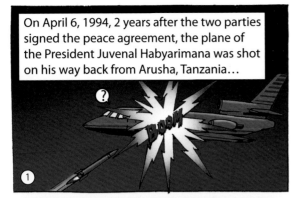

That night Theoneste Bagosora started the genocide of Tutsis who were in the country as planned, using Interahamwe and his soldiers…

Go and kill every Tutsi, starting with children in the womb. Kill everyone and do not forget the older people. We have to cleanse the country. If any Hutu tries to protect them, kill them as well.

The genocide was well planned. They had distributed guns to people. The death of the President was a sign to start. It was said that he was reluctant to allow the killing of everyone and so he became a victim as well. The UNAMIR did nothing, rather they pulled away their soldiers from the country. The scenes of horror were exactly as The Virgin Mary described on August 15, 1982…

Since the killing of the innocent started, the leader of the army of RPF Inkotanyi, called all the soldiers to get ready for a war to save the country…

If they are starting to kill innocent people, there is no more negotiations with the killers. We have an obligation to save Rwanda and we will bring the killers to justice.

Tutsis were killed in their homes, they were killed in the churches as they destroyed them. Some of the religious people killed as well and some are in prison to this day, as Jesus warned them trying to save them…

It took 3 months for the RPF Inkotanyi to stop the genocide. However when they arrived, more than a million Tutsis had been killed including Hutus who tried to protect them openly…

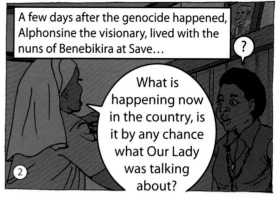

A few days after the genocide happened, Alphonsine the visionary, lived with the nuns of Benebikira at Save…

What is happening now in the country, is it by any chance what Our Lady was talking about?

Alphonsine was not happy to hear that some people still doubted…

So you never took it seriously, now you remember when it is too late. She told us and begged us to change and people doubted and here we are.

On April 1, 1994, the Virgin Mary appeared to Alphonsine privately…

In a few days, your country will undergo terrible things you never experienced before, pray a lot.

On January 12, 1994 Mary appeared to Anathalie in private as well…

Your country is about to fall into the darkest night.

Pray a lot so you will not fall.

On May 15, 1994 Mary appeared to Valentine Nyiramukiza who still has a public apparition every May 15…

This is what I have been trying to protect you from.

In 1992, the diocese of Butare was divided in 2 parts. Diocese of Butare and of Gikongoro. The Kibeho village became a part of Diocese of Gikongoro. It was given a new Bishop Augustin Misago and Bishop Jean Baptiste Gahamanyi kept the new Diocese of Butare…

On June 26, 2001 Bishop Misago invited both theology and medical commissions to announce to them his decisions of the Kibeho apparitions…

Yes the Virgin Mary appeared in Kibeho

And after my evalua-tion, I decided to only announce the approval of the 3 girls who were in the same school for the apparition of the Virgin Mary. Alphonsine, Anathalie and Marie Claire.

Your Excellency, you know very well, it is not only them who had apparitions. What about the others?

How about the apparitions of Jesus?

3 girls were accepted. Alphonsine Mumureke, today, 35 years later, lives in Italy as a nun. Anathalie Mukamazimpaka lives in Kibeho as Mary requested of her. Marie Claire Mukangango after school, she became a teacher, got married and was killed during the genocide against Tutsis in 1994 trying to save her husband…

So you accept the Virgin Mary's apparitions and not Jesus? But how do you explain to people about Anathalie's appari-tions of Jesus? Did she lie?

The apparitions of Jesus are complicated. There are not many people who saw Him in the world. I am not saying He didn't appear but I will come to that later, for now I will only announce 3 girls who lived with the nuns and their apparitions with Mary. That is all.

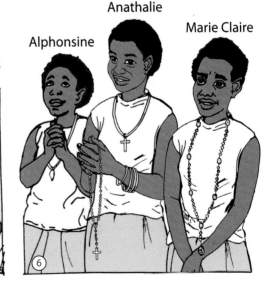

Anathalie

Alphonsine

Marie Claire

Segatashya also died during the genocide at the age of 28. As Jesus had predicted, he died before he was 33 years old. Those who followed his apparitions, continue to pray and hope that the church will acknowledge him…

Agnes survived the genocide, though they killed her whole family. Jesus had told her that she would survive. She lives in Butare near Kibeho and she continues to have private apparitions…

There is not much news about Stephanie, they said she died…

There is no news about Vestine Salima either. They say that she also died soon after the genocide…

Valentine lives in Belgium and she continues to have public apparitions of Mary every May 15. Jesus' public apparitions ended on March 20, 1993…

After the genocide, Rwandans have learned from their mistakes and though the country is still healing, it has recovered and is reconciling its people in the effort to never let what happened, happen again. Many say that Rwanda is now maybe the most peaceful country in Africa and it attracts a lot of tourists…

A few years later, Bishop Augustin Misago died due to a heart attack. And the Diocese of Gikongoro was given a new Shepherd, Bishop Celestin Hakizimana. The new Bishop is very well loved, a man of faith indeed, a hero who saved people during the genocide. However people expect a lot from him, that maybe he will reopen the investigation of Jesus' apparitions and of the other visionaries. They hope he will finally build the Chapels Mary requested 35 years ago, where she wanted them…

This is the body of Christ…

To this day every time during every Feast in Kibeho, especially on August 15, the day of the Assumption, when priests start giving a blessing of water, there is a gentle rain that follows and it is understood to be a blessing of the Virgin Mary as she did many times in the past…

After the genocide against Tutsis, every Rwandan who knew about the message and the prophecy of Kibeho, regrets not having listened to Mary's Prophecy. Many have come back to God. The new leaders are committed to fight against discrimination and divisiveness among Rwandans at all cost. Every refugee is allowed to come back to the country and if he or she doesn't find means to come back, the government helps them. Nobody writes their ethnic group anywhere anymore, everyone is a Rwandan…

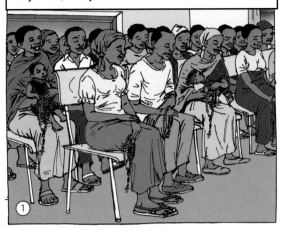

Kibeho has changed. Many religious orders have moved there to help people who come on pilgrimages. Kibeho is the first place to be approved by the Catholic Church in Africa to have Marian Apparitions even though many say Mary has visited every country in the world…

The school where the apparitions took place, has changed its name. It is called the High School of The Mother of the Word, the name The Virgin called herself when she appeared to Alphonsine Mumureke. The students wear blue and white uniforms, the colors worn by the Virgin when she appeared to Anathalie…

Many people now go to pray in Kibeho where many miracles are reported. Many healings are reported to occur among people who implore the Mother of God in this Holy place chosen by her to visit…

Among many prayers answered in Kibeho from around the world include those from people who have tried to conceive in vain; later they are blessed to give birth to children…

Others have prayed for their future love and God answered their prayers…

Many come to beg Mary to pray for them in order to find a job, and she helped them to find one…

There are others who decide to work for Our Lady of Kibeho and help her to spread and live the messages She gave in Kibeho. A group in the United States is especially growing…

Many friends of Our Lady of Kibeho around the world make retreats and hold conferences to share the message of Kibeho. Mary requested that we say the 7 Sorrows Rosary and teach it to others. She promised that those who will teach it, will receive special blessings…

The friends of Our Lady of Kibeho outside Rwanda continue to increase and they do charity work in Rwanda, especially after the genocide against Tutsis. They help the poor and support children to go to school…

There are also those who help take care of the orphans, providing food and clothes, in honor of Our Lady of Kibeho's request to care for the children…

Hail Mary, full of grace. The Lord is with you. Blessed are you among women, and blessed is the fruit of your womb, Jesus. Holy Mary Mother of God, pray for us sinners, now and at the hour of our death. Amen.

Mary's biggest wish is for every individual to change his/her heart and come back to God and pray more.

End